Gavin McNeill
Illustrations by Lauren McNeill

Periodic Table People

Bumblebee Books
London

Dedication

Written in celebration of the 150th anniversary
of Mendeleev's original Periodic Table of the
Elements in 1869.

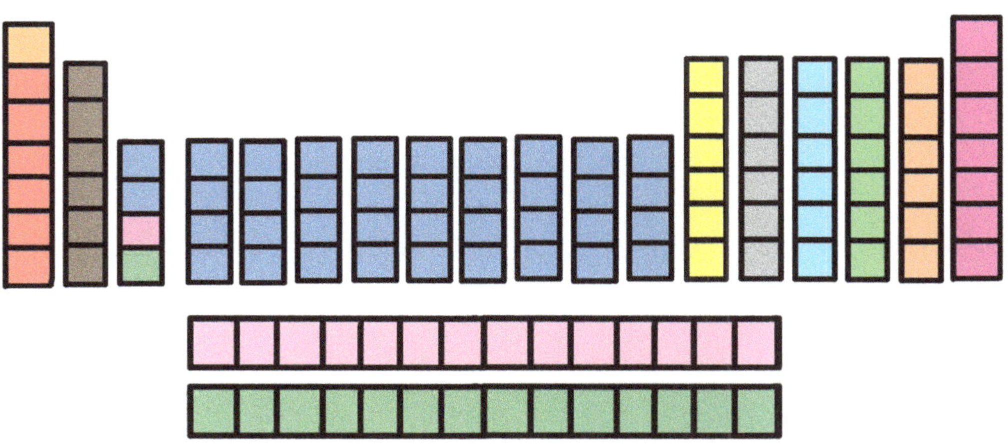

Imagine what would happen if the elements of the periodic table came alive. Each element would need a first name as well as using their element name as their surname.

Imagine if their first name was alliterative with their surname and they spent their time doing alliterative tasks.

This book personifies each of the 118 elements of the periodic table and will help you remember their names based on what they get up to e.g. Phil Phosphorus folds phones. For elements with unusual symbols, their name and activity reflects the symbol rather than the element names e.g. silver has the symbol Ag so Agatha Silver agitates silks.

This book has been written not only as an introduction to the elements of the periodic table, but also will help introduce new words, spelling and grammar to its readers.

Harry Hydrogen
highlights hydrants.

$^{1}_{1}\text{H}$

$^{4}_{2}\text{He}$

Helen Helium
helps heroes.

Lily Lithium
lifts lions.

$^{7}_{3}$Li

Beryl Beryllium berates berries.

$^{9}_{4}\text{Be}$

Bob Boron
bores bosses.

$^{11}_{5}\text{B}$

Carol Carbon
carries carrots.

$^{12}_{6}\text{C}$

Neville Nitrogen
neutralises nettles.

14
7 N

Oliver Oxygen oxidises oxen.

If these cattle lose electrons they'll become positively charged.

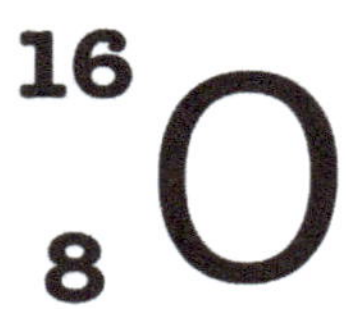

16
8 O

Fiona Fluorine
files flies.

19
9 F

Neil Neon
nears nets.

$^{20}_{10}$Ne

Nancy Sodium
nails socks.

23
11 Na

Maggie Magnesium magnifies magnets.

$^{24}_{12}$Mg

Alfie Aluminium
alters alloys.

27
13 Al

Simon Silicon
sifts silver.

28
14 Si

Phil Phosphorus
folds phones.

31
15 P

Sofia Sulfur
saves scarves.

32
S
16

Clive Chlorine classifies clocks.

35.5
17
Cl

Archie Argon
arranges aardvarks.

$^{40}_{18}\text{Ar}$

Kerry Potassium
keeps potatoes.

39
K
19

Calvin Calcium
calls calendars.

40
20 Ca

Scarlet Scandium
scares scarecrows.

45
21 Sc

Titus Titanium
types titles.

48
22 Ti

Valerie Vanadium values vans.

Craig Chromium creates crates.

$^{52}_{24}$Cr

Mandy Manganese
manages mangoes.

Felicity Iron
feels irons.

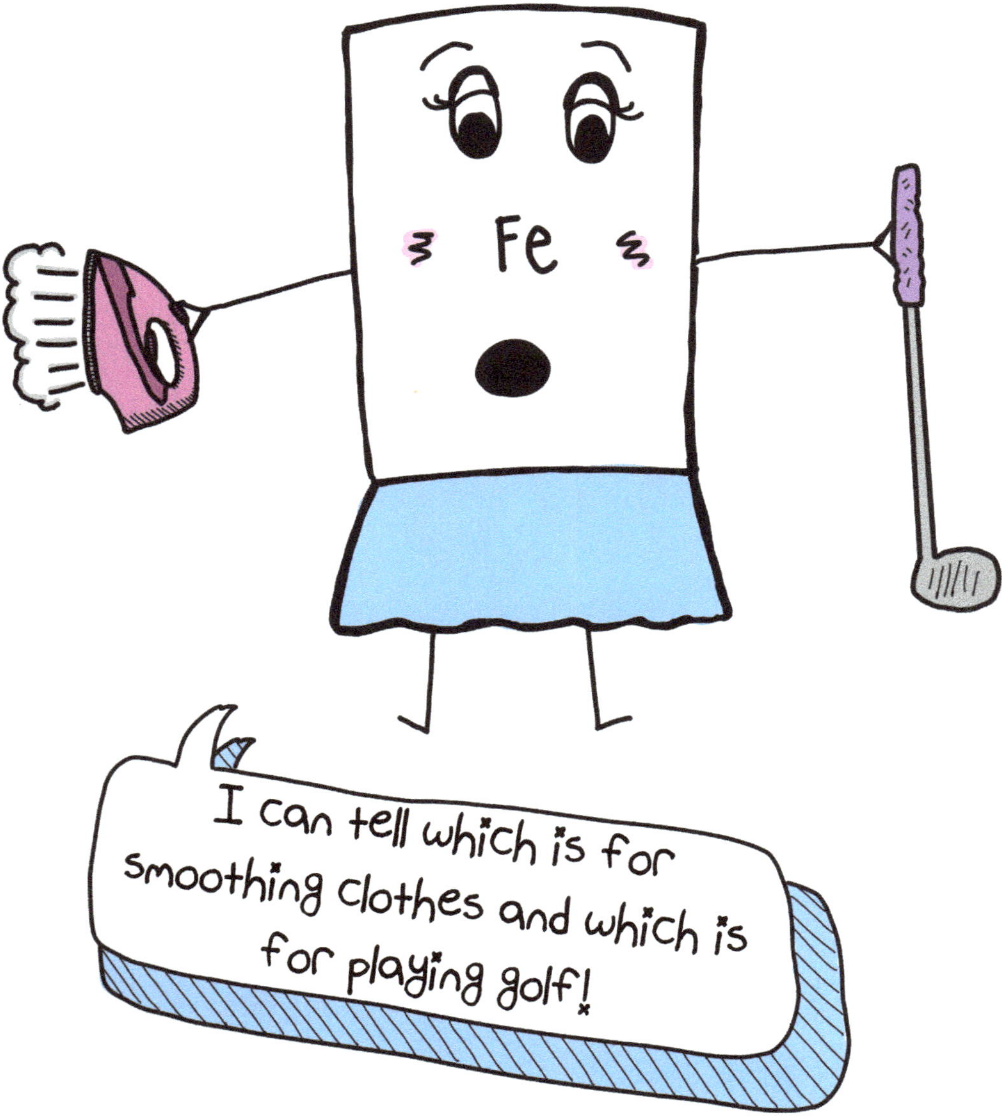

Cody Cobalt counts
cookies.

$^{59}_{27}$Co

Nicola Nickel
nicks nickels.

59
28 Ni

Cuba Copper
copies cops.

63.5
29
Cu

Zane Zinc
zones zebras.

65
30 Zn

Gavin Gallium
galvanises gates.

$^{70}_{31}$Ga

Gerald Germanium gets gerbils.

73
32 Ge

Asa Arsenic assists arsonists.

75
33 As

Selena Selenium sells seashells.

79
34 Se

Brian Bromine
brings bread.

Kris Krypton
craves krill.

84
36 Kr

Robbie Rubidium
robs rubbers.

85
37 Rb

Sarah Strontium
straightens streets.

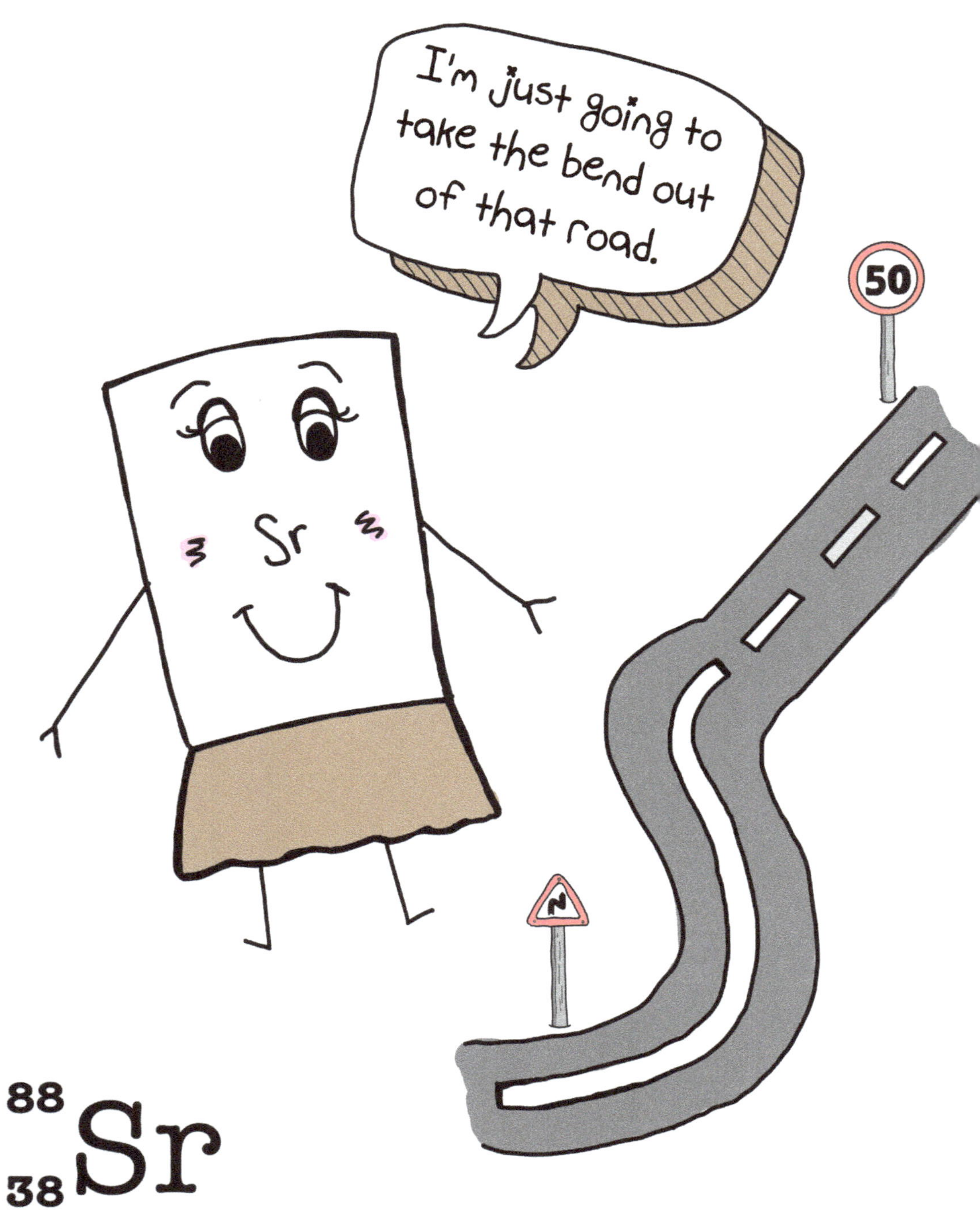

$^{88}_{38}$Sr

Yvonne Yttrium
eats eels.

89 Y
39

Zorro Zirconium
sorts sorbets.

91
40
Zr

Nobby Niobium nabs nibs.

93
41 Nb

96
42 Mo

Molly Molybdenum mows molehills.

If I follow these drops of acid, I might find the people who help science teachers.
Tc

$^{97}_{43}\text{Tc}$

Ruth Ruthenium
rubs rust.

101
44 Ru

Rhona Rhodium
relishes radishes.

Paddy Palladium
paddles pals.

106
46 Pd

Agatha Silver agitates silks.

108
47 Ag

Cedric Cadmium codes Cadillacs.

$^{112}_{48}$Cd

Ian Indium
indicates instructions.

$^{115}_{49}$In

Stanley Tin
standardises tins.

$^{119}_{50}$Sn

Sebastian Antimony
stabs ants.

Terry Tellurium tells tales.

128
52 Te

Imogen Iodine
idolises ions.

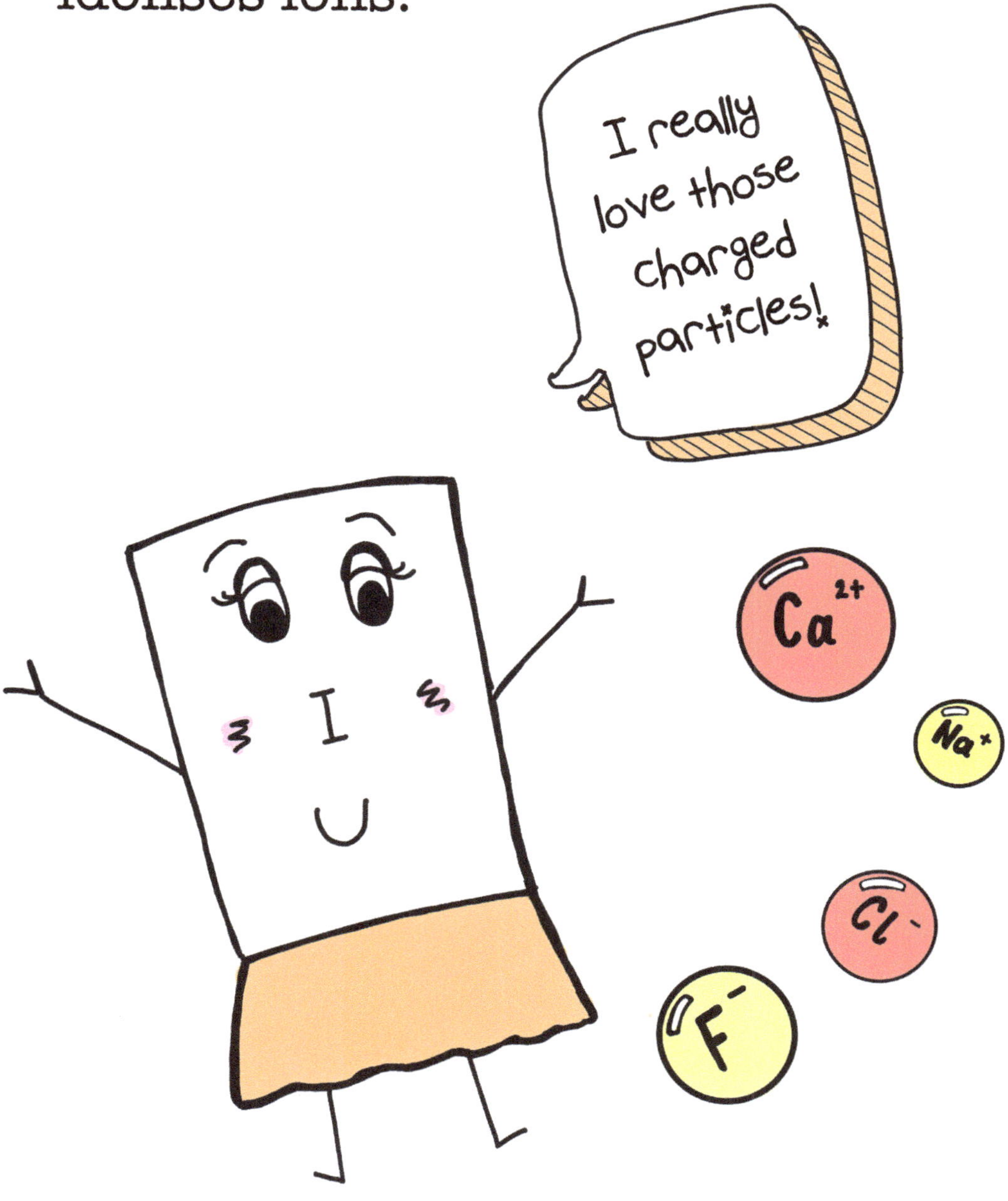

Xander Xenon
expects excellence.

I want to see the best in everything you do!
Xe
131
54 Xe

Cassandra Caesium causes chaos.

Barbara barium
bares barriers.

$^{137}_{56}$Ba

Larry Lanthanum lassoes lamps.

139
57
La

Celine Cerium
celebrates celery.

140
58 Ce

Peter Praseodymium
pares pears.

$^{141}_{59}$ Pr

Noddy Neodymium
needs noodles.

144
60 Nd

Pamela Promethium promotes prams.

145
61 Pm

$^{150}_{\ 62}$Sm

Sam Samarium
samples samphire.

Eunice Europium
unites Europeans.

152
63 Eu

Gordon Gadolinium
goads gods.

157
64 Gd

Tabitha Terbium terrorises terrapins.

159
65
Tb

Dylan Dysprosium dyes diamonds.

$^{162}_{66}$Dy

Holly Holmium
holds holes.

$^{165}_{67}$Ho

Eric Erbium erases errors.

$^{167}_{68}\text{Er}$

Tim Thulium
times tomatoes.

169
69

Tm

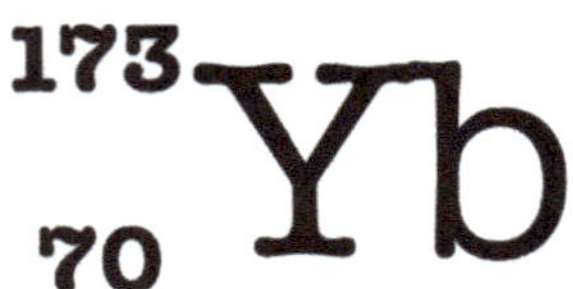

$^{173}_{70}$Yb

Ysobel Ytterbium italicises initials.

Lucy Lutetium
lures lutes.

175
71 Lu

Hafna Hafnium halves hairs.

Hf
Each 20cm length of hair needs to be cut into two equal 10cm lengths.

178
72 Hf

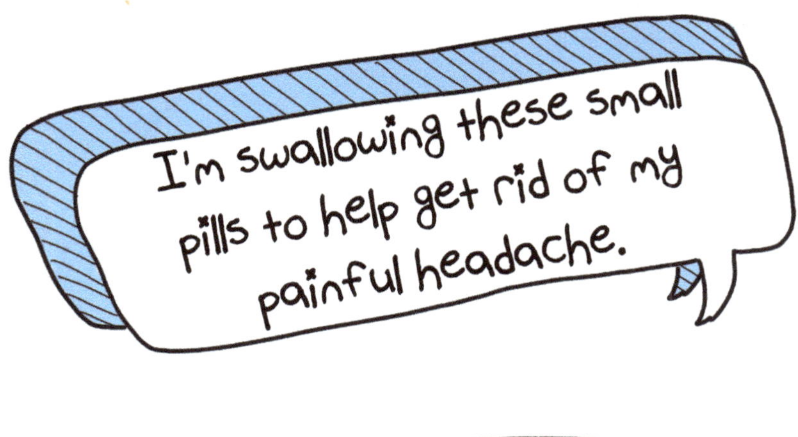

Tamsin Tantalum takes tablets.

181
73 Ta

Wolfgang Tungsten
tugs wolves.

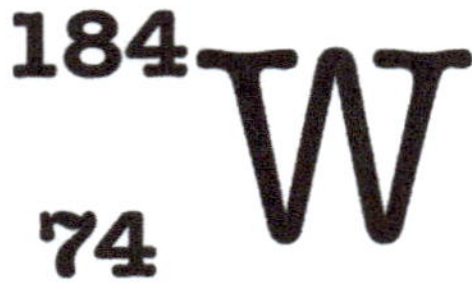

184
W
74

Rebecca Rhenium reads references.

186
75 Re

190
76
Os

Ossie Osmium
ostracises ostriches.

Iris Iridium
irons irises.

192
77 Ir

Patrick Platinum
plays pots.

$^{195}_{78}$Pt

Audrey Gold
authorises goals.

197
79 Au

201
80 Hg

Hugo Mercury hugs mermaids.

Thalia Thallium
thrills thimbles.

204
81 Tl

Pablo Lead
publishes leads.

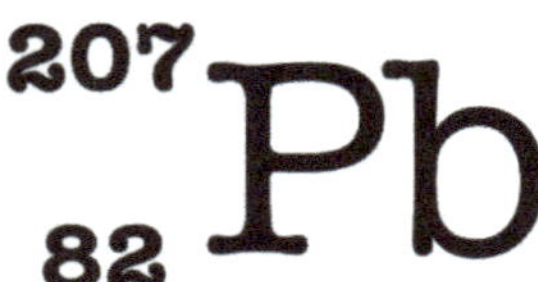

$^{207}_{82}\text{Pb}$

Billy Bismuth
builds bins.

209
83
Bi

Polly Polonium
posts potatoes.

Astrid Astatine
astounds astronauts.

222
86 Rn

Ronnie Radon
rents radios.

Frank Francium
franks freezers.

223
87
Fr

226
88 Ra

Ray Radium
radiates radiation.

Ace Actinium accepts actors.

227
89 Ac

Thomas Thorium
thinks thoughts.

$^{232}_{90}$Th

Priscilla Protactinium protects protons.

$^{231}_{91}$Pa

$^{238}_{92}\text{U}$

Ursula Uranium
uses utensils.

Napoleon Neptunium nips napes.

237
93 Np

Paul Plutonium
plucks poultry.

$$^{244}_{94}\text{Pu}$$

Amy Americium amuses amphibians.

$^{243}_{95}$Am

Cameron Curium cures camels.

$$^{247}_{96}\text{Cm}$$

Becky Berkelium breaks bricks.

$^{247}_{97}$ Bk

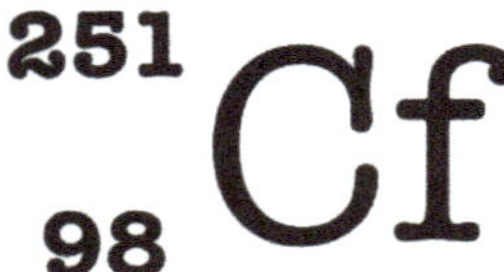

$^{251}_{\ 98}$Cf

Clifford Californium
calibrates coffees.

Esme Einsteinium estimates estuaries.

$^{252}_{99}\text{Es}$

257
100 Fm

Femi Fermium
frames females.

Maud Mendelevium mends mandolins.

259
102
No

Norman Nobelium notices gnomes.

Lauren Lawrencium
launders lorries.

262
103 Lr

Rufus Rutherfordium
raffles rafts.

267
104 Rf

Debbie Dubnium dubs dabs.

270
105
Db

Sigourney Seaborgium
suggests sage.

269
106 Sg

Beth Bohrium
borrows borders.

270
107 Bh

Hassan Hassium
has haslet.

270
108 Hs

Matthew Meitnerium matches mats.

278
109 Mt

Daisy Darmstadtium dates darts.

281
110 Ds

Roger Roentgenium
registers rugs.

281
111 Rg

Colin Copernicium
connects cones.

285
112 Cn

Nicholas Nihonium
nibbles nightwear.

286
113 Nh

289
114 **Fl**

Florence Flerovium flies flags.

Michael Moscovium microchips mice.

Liv Livermorium
loves Liverpool.

293
116 Lv

Tessa Tennessine
tenses tendons.

293
117
Ts

Olga Oganesson organises organisms.

294
118 Og

Explaining the Science

Each element's nose is its chemical symbol, which is either just one capital letter or a capital letter followed by a lowercase letter, e.g. C for carbon, Co for cobalt. Some symbols relate to the element's name in a language other than English, e.g. sodium is Na which comes from the Latin word "natrium". The symbol is also shown at the bottom of the page, with the element's atomic number acting as the page number. The upper number is the mass number which relates to how heavy each element is.

The colour of the shorts or skirt of each element relates to its position in the periodic table. There are eight vertical groups which each contain elements that have similar chemical properties. The three horizontal blocks in the centre are called the Transition Metals, Lanthanides and Actinides.

Explaining the Literacy

Each page contains a four-word sentence. The first two words are proper nouns, which are words that are names: a boy's or girl's first name followed by the element name. The third word is a verb (a doing word) and they are all the third person singular in the present tense so always end in the letter 's'. The fourth word is a plural noun (an object word) so also (usually) it ends in the letter 's'.

Alliterations are sentences which contain words that start with the same phonic sound. Each element's sentence is alliterative with either the element's name or its chemical symbol.

About the Author

Gavin McNeill is Head of Chemistry at a secondary school in Cheshire, who has a passion for teaching young people about the chemical elements. He even designs his own versions of the periodic table, using the symbols of the elements as a basis for topics such as the periodic table of animals, musical instruments, artists, sports stars and many more.

His daughter Lauren McNeill is also a teacher, of maths at a secondary school in Halton, who uses her artistic and creative skills to help educate young people.

www.ingramcontent.com/pod-product-compliance
Lightning Source LLC
Chambersburg PA
CBHW050006040726
47599CB00014B/1240